**ACCOUNTING LIFEP**

PAYROLL ACCOUNTING, TAXE

CONTENTS

Author: **Daniel L. Ritzman, B.S.**
Editors: Alan Christopherson, M.S.
                                                  Jennifer L. Davis, B.S.

Alpha Omega Publications®

804 N. 2nd Ave. E., Rock Rapids, IA 51246-1759
© MM by Alpha Omega Publications, Inc.   All rights reserved.
LIFEPAC is a registered trademark of Alpha Omega Publications, Inc.

All trademarks and/or service marks referenced in this material are the property of their respective owners. Alpha Omega Publications, Inc. makes no claim of ownership to any trademarks and/or service marks other than their own and their affiliates', and makes no claim of affiliation to any companies whose trademarks may be listed in this material, other than their own.

ACCOUNTING LIFEPAC 9
PAYROLL ACCOUNTING, TAXES & REPORTS

OVERVIEW

In LIFEPAC 8 you learned about various types of **payroll deduction**s, calculating employee earnings and keeping payroll records. This LIFEPAC® is designed to help you understand how to analyze, journalize and post payroll transactions. It also discusses the responsibilities of the employer to accurately report and pay the federal and state payroll taxes withheld from his employees' **wages**.

Recording the payment of the payroll involves maintaining payroll records and then recording the payroll expenses and liabilities for each **pay period**. The bookkeeper must also determine the employer's payroll tax liability and complete federal and state payroll tax reports.

OBJECTIVES

When you have completed this LIFEPAC you will be able to:

1. Recognize the accounting concepts and practices related to payroll accounts, taxes, and reports.

2. Analyze payroll transactions.

3. Journalize the payroll transactions.

4. Post the payroll transactions.

5. Describe the employer payroll taxes.

6. Record the employer payroll taxes.

7. Prepare payroll tax reports.

VOCABULARY

Employee Earnings Record – a form used to summarize payroll deductions and payments made to each individual employee.

Federal Unemployment Tax Act (FUTA) – a federal tax used for administration of state and federal unemployment programs.

Federal Insurance Contribution Act (FICA) – a law requiring employers and employees to pay taxes to the federal government to support the Social Security programs; the term "FICA" is also used to refer to the taxes themselves.

Merit Rating – a rating used to adjust an employer's state unemployment tax liability based upon a record of steady employment.

Pay Period – a period covered by a salary payment.

Payroll – all salaries and wages paid to employees.

Payroll Deductions – required and voluntary deductions from gross earnings to determine net pay.

Payroll Register – an accounting form that summarizes payroll information for all employees during a specific pay period.

Salary – a specified amount paid to an employee per month or per year.

State Unemployment Tax – a tax imposed by a state to pay benefits to the unemployed.

Wages – payment based on an hourly rate or a piecework basis.

SECTION I. ANALYZING & RECORDING PAYROLL TRANSACTIONS

Payroll Records

Employers are required by law to keep payroll records on their employees for a period of at least four years. These payroll records should include: (1) the **salary** or **wage** amounts paid; (2) the amounts deducted from the employees' earnings; (3) the expenses involved with the payroll; and (4) the payroll taxes paid by the employer and the employees to the government. The **payroll register** that you studied in LIFEPAC 8 summarizes this payroll data for the employees of a business by itemizing their total earnings and payroll deductions.

The totals of the columns in the payroll register are also the basis for the journal entries to record the payroll. The information obtained from the register is not posted directly to the general ledger accounts, however. The payroll entry must first be recorded in the general journal and then posted to the general ledger accounts.

The additional employer's tax liabilities are also recorded in the journal. The general ledger is used to summarize total earnings and deductions for all employees. The individual employee earnings record provides a summary of each employee's earnings and deductions per pay period. Thus the payroll register and **employee earnings records** provide all the payroll information needed to prepare a payroll and payroll tax reports.

On certain dates, the employer must send the amounts withheld from employees' earnings for taxes (mandatory deductions) to the federal and state governments. Other deductions such as union dues, group health insurance and savings plans (voluntary deductions) must also be paid to their respective agencies or organizations. Until these amounts are paid, they represent liabilities.

Analyzing the Payroll Entry

The debit and credit amounts to record the payment of payroll in the journal are obtained from the column totals of the payroll register.

PAYROLL REGISTER for the Semimonthly Payroll Period Ended *December 31, 20—*

NO.	NAME	MARITAL STATUS	EXEMP.	REGULAR	OVERTIME	TOTAL	FEDERAL INCOME TAX	FICA	MEDICARE	TOTAL DEDUCTIONS	AMOUNT
		EMPLOYEE DATA		EARNINGS			DEDUCTIONS				NET PAY
3	Jones, Mildred	S	1	800 00		800 00	87 00	49 60	11 60	148 20	651 80
1	King, Mary	S	1	750 00	50 00	800 00	87 00	49 60	11 60	148 20	651 80
2	Lowe, Howard	M	2	250 00		250 00	0 00	15 50	3 63	19 13	230 87
4	Martin, John	M	1	695 00		695 00	46 00	43 09	10 08	99 17	595 83
5	Ness, Elton	S	0	185 00		185 00	11 00	11 47	2 68	25 15	159 85
	Totals			2680 00		2730 00	231 00	169 26	39 59	439 85	2290 15
						1	**2**	**3**	**4**		**5**

1. Wages and salaries are a business expense. The account that reflects this expense is Salary Expense, which has a debit balance; therefore, Salary Expense will be debited.

What does this total represent?	The salary expense for the pay period
Which account is affected?	Salary Expense
What journal entry is made?	Debit Salary Expense for $2,730.00

2. The $231.00 for federal income tax withheld becomes a liability to the business until the taxes are deposited with the federal government. Record the liability by crediting Employee Income Tax Payable. Liabilities increase on the credit side.

What does this total represent?	The amount owed to the government for income tax for the pay period
Which account is affected?	Employee Income Tax Payable
What journal entry is made?	Credit Employee Income Tax Payable for $231.00

3. The FICA tax total of $169.26 also represents a liability for the pay period. (NOTE: Some businesses show a combined withholding amount for FICA and Medicare. Others list them separately because both taxes have different bases. They are both reported, along with income tax withheld, on the same Form 941 – Employer's Quarterly Federal Tax Return.)

What does this total represent?	The amount owed to the government for employees' FICA tax for the pay period
Which account is affected?	FICA Tax Payable
What journal entry is made?	Credit FICA Tax Payable for $169.26

4. The total deduction of $39.59 for Medicare tax is a liability until the tax is deposited at the end of the quarter. Record the liability by crediting Medicare Tax Payable.

What does this total represent?	The total employees' Medicare tax for the pay period
Which account is affected?	Medicare Tax Payable
What journal entry is made?	Credit Medicare Tax Payable for $39.59

5. The business draws a check (which becomes the source document for the journal entry to record payroll) for the net pay total of $2,290.15 from the general checking account. This amount is then deposited in a special payroll account from which individual payroll checks are written. Since Cash is an asset account with a debit balance, the account decreases on the credit side.

What does this total represent?	The amount actually paid to the employees for the pay period
Which account is affected?	Cash
What journal entry is made?	Credit Cash for $2,290.15

The T accounts below illustrate at a glance how these various accounts are affected. They also show the equality of the debit and credit amounts in this transaction.

Journalizing the Payroll Entry

The journal entry to record the payroll for this pay period is shown below:

JOURNAL						Page 2	
Date 20—	Account Title and Explanation	Doc No.	Post. Ref.	General Debit		General Credit	
Dec. 31	Salary Expense			2730	00		
	Employee Income Tax Pay.					231	00
	FICA Tax Payable					169	26
	Medicare Tax Payable					39	59
	Cash	Ck 120				2290	15

Remember that Salary Expense is always debited with the amount of total earnings and Cash is always credited with the amount of net pay.

Posting the Payroll Entry

After the payroll has been journalized, the entry must be posted. (NOTE: Since the December 31 payroll is the second payroll for the month, the accounts will have previous balances.)

Account Title: *Cash*   **Account No.** *110*

Date 20—		Explanation	Post. Ref.	Debit		Credit		Balance			
								Debit		Credit	
Dec.	18		✔					5000	00		
	31		J2			2290	15	2709	85		

Account Title: *Employee Income Tax Payable*   **Account No.** *210*

Date 20—		Explanation	Post. Ref.	Debit		Credit		Balance			
								Debit		Credit	
Dec.	15		✔							231	00
	31		J2			231	00			462	00

Account Title: *FICA Tax Payable*   **Account No.** *220*

Date 20—		Explanation	Post. Ref.	Debit		Credit		Balance			
								Debit		Credit	
Dec.	15		✔							338	52
	31		J2			169	26			507	78

Account Title: *Medicare Tax Payable*   **Account No.** *230*

Date 20—		Explanation	Post. Ref.	Debit		Credit		Balance			
								Debit		Credit	
Dec.	15		✔							79	18
	31		J2			39	59			118	77

Account Title: *Salary Expense*   **Account No.** *570*

Date 20—		Explanation	Post. Ref.	Debit		Credit		Balance			
								Debit		Credit	
Dec.	31		J2	2730	00			2730	00		

Complete the following activity.

1.1 Use the information on the payroll register below to journalize the payroll transactions for the pay period ending January 15 of the current year, Ck 132.

PAYROLL REGISTER for the Semimonthly Payroll Period Ended *January 15, 20—*

NO.	NAME	MARITAL STATUS	EXEMP.	REGULAR	OVERTIME	TOTAL	FEDERAL INCOME TAX	FICA	MEDICARE	TOTAL DEDUCTIONS	AMOUNT
3	Bates, Mary	m	3	700 00		700 00	14 00	43 40	10 15	67 55	632 45
1	Clark, Chris	S	1	100 00		100 00	0 00	6 20	1 45	7 65	92 35
2	Jones, Harry	m	3	700 00	50 00	750 00	20 00	46 50	10 88	77 38	672 62
4	Jones, Mildred	S	1	800 00		800 00	87 00	49 60	11 60	148 20	651 80
9	King, Mary	S	1	800 00		800 00	87 00	49 60	11 60	148 20	651 80
6	Lowe, Howard	m	2	250 00		250 00	0 00	15 50	3 63	19 13	230 87
8	Martin, John	m	1	695 00		695 00	46 00	43 09	10 08	99 17	595 83
7	Ness, Elton	S	0	185 00		185 00	12 00	11 47	2 68	26 15	158 85
5	Zybrinski, Carol	S	1	600 00	22 50	622 50	60 00	38 60	9 03	107 63	514 87
	Totals			4830 00	72 50	4902 50	326 00	303 96	71 10	701 06	4201 44

| | | EARNINGS | | | DEDUCTIONS | | | | NET PAY |

JOURNAL Page *3*

Date	Account Title and Explanation	Doc No.	Post. Ref.	General Debit	General Credit

Complete the following activity.

1.2 From the journal entry on the previous page, post the payroll transactions for the pay period ending January 15 of the current year.

Account Title: Cash Account No. 110

Date 20—		Explanation	Post. Ref.	Debit		Credit		Balance			
								Debit		Credit	
Jan.	1		✔	7871	00			7871	00		

Account Title: Employee Income Tax Payable Account No. 210

Date 20—		Explanation	Post. Ref.	Debit		Credit		Balance			
								Debit		Credit	

Account Title: FICA Tax Payable Account No. 220

Date 20—		Explanation	Post. Ref.	Debit		Credit		Balance			
								Debit		Credit	

Account Title: Medicare Tax Payable Account No. 230

Date 20—		Explanation	Post. Ref.	Debit		Credit		Balance			
								Debit		Credit	

Account Title: Salary Expense Account No. 570

Date 20—		Explanation	Post. Ref.	Debit		Credit		Balance			
								Debit		Credit	

Review the material in this section in preparation for the Self Test. The Self Test will check your mastery of this particular section. The items missed on this Self Test will indicate specific areas where restudy is needed for mastery.

SELF TEST 1

Match the following accounting terms with their definitions (each answer, 2 points).

1.01 _____ a period covered by a salary or wage payment

1.02 _____ payment based on an hourly rate or a piece-work basis

1.03 _____ required and voluntary amounts taken from gross earnings to determine net pay

1.04 _____ all salaries and wages paid to employees

1.05 _____ a tax used for administration of state and federal unemployment programs

1.06 _____ a tax used to support social security programs

1.07 _____ a form used to summarize payroll deductions and payments made to each individual employee

1.08 _____ an accounting form that summarizes payroll information for all employees during a specific pay period

1.09 _____ a specified amount paid to an employee per month or per year

a. salary

b. wage

c. employee earnings record

d. payroll register

e. FICA

f. journalizing

g. FUTA

h. payroll

i. pay period

j. payroll deductions

k. withholding allowance

Answer the following questions (each answer, 5 points).

1.010 What is included in the payroll records employers are required to keep for four years?

a. _____

b. _____

c. _____

d. _____

1.011 Why do the amounts withheld from employees' earnings become liabilities to the employer?

_____

_____

9

PAYROLL REGISTER for the Semimonthly Payroll Period Ended *December 31, 20—*

NO.	NAME	MARITAL STATUS	EXEMP.	REGULAR	OVERTIME	TOTAL	FEDERAL INCOME TAX	FICA	MEDICARE	TOTAL DEDUCTIONS	NET PAY AMOUNT
					EARNINGS			DEDUCTIONS			NET PAY
3	Jones, Mildred	S	1	800 00		800 00	87 00	49 60	11 60	148 20	651 80
1	King, Mary	S	1	750 00	50 00	800 00	87 00	49 60	11 60	148 20	651 80
2	Lowe, Howard	M	2	250 00		250 00	0 00	15 50	3 63	19 13	230 87
4	Martin, John	M	1	695 00		695 00	46 00	43 09	10 08	99 17	595 83
5	Ness, Elton	S	0	185 00		185 00	11 00	11 47	2 68	25 15	159 85
	Totals			2680 00		2730 00	231 00	169 26	39 59	439 85	2290 15
						1.012	**1.013**	**1.014**	**1.015**		**1.016**

Analyze the transactions to journalize the payroll entry from the payroll register shown above (each answer, 3 points).

1.012 a. What does this total represent? _____

_____

b. Which account is affected? _____

c. What journal entry is made? _____

1.013 a. What does this total represent? _____

_____

b. Which account is affected? _____

c. What journal entry is made? _____

1.014 a. What does this total represent? _____

_____

b. Which account is affected? _____

c. What journal entry is made? _____

1.015 a. What does this total represent? _____

_____

b. Which account is affected? _____

c. What journal entry is made? _____

1.016 a. What does this total represent? _____

_____

b. Which account is affected? _____

c. What journal entry is made? _____

70
/
88

Score _____

Adult Check _____

Initial   Date

SECTION II. DETERMINING EMPLOYER PAYROLL TAXES

FICA Taxes

All employers must pay payroll taxes. Each employer is responsible to pay the federal government the income tax and the employee's portion of FICA taxes withheld from their salaries. These taxes are liabilities to the business until paid to the government.

Employers must also pay four separate payroll taxes in addition to what is withheld from the employees' wages. These taxes are: (1) Employer's matching FICA tax, (2) Employer's matching Medicare tax, (3) Federal unemployment tax, and (4) State unemployment tax.

You learned in LIFEPAC 8 that not only are employees liable for Social Security taxes, but the employer must also contribute to the funds at the same rate as the employee. Therefore, the employer must pay 6.2% for FICA tax and 1.45% for Medicare tax on each employee's total earnings *in addition to the amounts he withholds from employees' earnings.* These employer payroll taxes are expenses to the business. The tax rates in this unit were current when the material was written. Although the rates may have changed the computational process remains the same.

The FICA tax rate is set by Congress. This rate applies both to the employee and the employer. As earnings increase and retirement distribution grows, Congress may change the tax rate and the tax base. The FICA tax, as you will recall, is a combination of both Social Security and Medicare taxes. Since these taxes have different tax bases, many businesses calculate each as a separate tax. This method eliminates supporting documents showing how each tax was calculated for each individual on the payroll.

Tax	Tax Rate	Max. Taxable Earnings
Social Security (FICA): retirement, survivor's and disability benefits	6.2%	$76,200.00
Medicare	1.45%	No Limit
Total	7.65%	

The Social Security and Medicare taxes are the only taxes paid by both the employer and the employee.

FUTA Tax

The **Federal Unemployment Tax Act (FUTA)** levies a payroll tax on employers of one or more employees. The payroll tax is levied only on employers and is based upon the total earnings of each employee. The regulation states that the money will be used to administer state unemployment programs— not to pay benefits. During periods of high unemployment, however, the federal government has loaned states funds from the FUTA accounts.

The Federal Unemployment Tax Act was passed in 1935 with two major purposes: (1) To encourage states to create an unemployment insurance fund within their own governmental structure, and (2) To provide any necessary funds to help states administer their unemployment insurance programs (payment of benefits to unemployed workers, job search facilities and other job-related services). Today FUTA's major functions are to help the states with administrative costs and to have a measure of control over state programs.

FUTA Requirements for Employers:

1. Pay FUTA tax of 6.2% of the first $7,000.00 in wages paid each to employee. The law grants a credit of 5.4% to employers in any state that provides a state unemployment tax program. Since all states now provide unemployment tax programs, the net federal tax is .8%.

2. Report the amount of the tax liability by filing a tax return. This return is called Employer's Annual Federal Unemployment Tax Return, Form 940. This return must be filed by January 31st following the end of each tax year.

3. Keep records to substantiate the information on the tax return. Normally, required payroll records and accounting records satisfy this regulation.

4. Timely deposits must be made. A quarterly deposit must be made if the total FUTA tax for the quarter is greater than $100.00. If no quarterly deposits are required, the total tax due must be paid by January 31st following the end of the tax year.

Calculating FUTA Taxable Earnings. The FUTA tax is based upon accumulated earnings. Once an employee's accumulated earnings exceed $7,000.00, his earnings are exempt from FUTA tax (see the table and explanation on the following page). The accumulated earnings figure is found on the employee earnings record.

Determine the sum total of all taxable earnings and apply the federal unemployment tax rate of .8% to arrive at the employer's federal unemployment tax liability.

Employee	Accumulated Earnings 11/30/20–	Current Earnings 12/15/20–	Unemployment Taxable Earnings
Jones, Mildred	$9,200.00	$800.00	$ 0.00
King, Mary	6,400.00	800.00	600.00
Lowe, Howard	4,890.00	450.00	450.00
Martin, John	11,690.00	695.00	0.00
Ness, Elton	5,840.00	185.00	185.00

Total: $1,235.00

Steps to Find Taxable Earnings:

Mildred Jones Since Mildred's accumulated earnings of $9,200.00 exceed $7,000.00, her current earnings are not subject to federal unemployment tax.

Mary King Mary's accumulated earnings are under $7,000.00; however, the addition of her current earnings will put her over the $7,000.00 limit ($7,200.00); therefore, $600.00 of her current earnings are subject to federal unemployment tax.

Howard Lowe Since Howard's accumulated earnings of $4,890.00 do not exceed $7,000.00, all of his current earnings are subject to federal unemployment tax.

John Martin Since John's accumulated earnings exceed $7,000.00, his current earnings are not subject to federal unemployment tax.

Elton Ness Since Elton's accumulated earnings of $5,840.00 do not exceed $7,000.00, all of his current earnings are subject to federal unemployment tax.

The employer's federal unemployment tax is then calculated as follows:

Unemployment Taxable Earnings of $1,235.00 X .8% = $9.88 tax owed on the 12/15 payroll

State Unemployment Tax

All states maintain their unemployment insurance programs by levying a payroll tax on employers. Although the state unemployment tax rate varies among states, it is usually applied to the first $7,000.00 earned by each employee. To determine the exact tax rate that must be paid by each employer, the state calculates the employer's **merit rating**. This merit rating depends upon the number of employees that are laid off during slack seasons. If the employer lay-off rate is low, the employees will not have to collect unemployment benefits. Fewer layoffs means a better merit rating for the employer.

Each employer must submit an unemployment tax report. These reports must be filed and taxes paid within one month after the end of each calendar quarter. The tax return usually includes the name of the employee and the employee's wages.

In addition to maintaining payroll records on each individual employee, the employer must keep a record of (1) date of employment or reinstatement, (2) date of termination, and (3) reason for termination.

Objectives of State Unemployment Insurance Programs:

1. *To pay unemployment benefits for stated time periods to unemployed individuals.* To be eligible, the employee must have worked for an employer who was required to pay unemployment insurance benefits.

2. *To stabilize employment by covered employers.* This is accomplished by the establishment of employer's merit ratings. These ratings are used to adjust the employer's tax liability based upon a record of steady employment.

3. *To establish and operate facilities that assist the unemployed in finding suitable employment and to help employers find employees.*

The procedure for calculating state unemployment tax is the same as the federal unemployment tax—accumulated employee earnings over $7,000.00 are exempt from state unemployment tax.

Employee	Accumulated Earnings 11/30/20–	Current Earnings 12/15/20–	Unemployment Taxable Earnings
Jones, Mildred	$9,200.00	$800.00	$ 0.00
King, Mary	6,400.00	800.00	600.00
Lowe, Howard	4,890.00	450.00	450.00
Martin, John	11,690.00	695.00	0.00
Ness, Elton	5,840.00	185.00	185.00

Total: $1,235.00

As mentioned earlier, an employer's state unemployment tax rate is usually based on a merit rating. We will assume that the employer of the above individuals has a merit rating of 5.4%. We will use this 5.4% rate to calculate the employer's state unemployment tax liability as follows:

Unemployment Taxable Earnings of $1,235.00 X 5.4% = $66.69 tax owed on the 12/15 payroll

Journalizing Payroll Taxes

The employer's matching FICA/Medicare taxes and the federal and state unemployment compensation taxes are expenses for the employer. Instead of keeping a separate account for each type of expense, they usually are combined into one account, Payroll Taxes Expense.

Although payroll taxes are reported quarterly, they are journalized at the end of each payroll period. The amounts to be recorded are as follows:

Employer's matching FICA tax	$169.26
Employer's matching Medicare tax	39.59
Unemployment tax – federal	9.88
Unemployment tax – state	66.69
Total payroll taxes expense	$285.42

As you recall from Section I, the source document for the journal entry to record the payroll was the check written from the general checking account to the payroll checking account. This check was for the total of the net pay column shown on the payroll register.

However, the payroll tax amounts shown above come from a number of different sources. The matching FICA and Medicare tax amounts come from the column totals in the payroll register, but the unemployment tax amounts are calculated only on the first $7,000.00 of accumulated earnings of each employee. The information on accumulated earnings is found in each employee's individual earnings record. This information can be gathered and summarized by the bookkeeper or payroll clerk in the form of an interoffice memo, giving the required information much like it has been presented above. This information can also be recorded on a form similar to the one shown below. The summary sheet (or memo) then becomes the source document for the journal entry to record payroll taxes.

Payroll Tax Summary Sheet		Memo #___4__
	Debit	*Credit*
Payroll Taxes Expense	$ 285.42	
FICA Tax Payable		$ 169.29
Medicare Tax Payable		39.59
Unemployment Tax Payable – Federal		9.88
Unemployment Tax Payable – State		66.69

Date 20—		Account Title and Explanation	Doc. No.	Post. Ref.	General Debit		General Credit	
Dec.	31	Payroll Taxes Expense			1 285	42		
		FICA Tax Payable					2 169	26
		Medicare Tax Payable					3 39	59
		Unempl. Tax Pay.–Federal					4 9	88
		Unempl. Tax Pay.–State	M4				5 66	69

1. The total payroll taxes of $285.42 represent an expense to the business for the pay period. The account that reflects this expense is Payroll Taxes Expense, which has a debit balance; therefore, Payroll Taxes Expense will be debited.

What is happening?	Payroll taxes are an expense of doing business
Which account is affected?	Payroll Taxes Expense
What journal entry is made?	Debit Payroll Taxes Expense for $285.42

2. The $169.26 for the employer's *matching* FICA funds becomes a liability to the business until the taxes are paid. Record the liability by crediting FICA Tax Payable. Liabilities increase on the credit side.

What is happening?	The amount of FICA tax owed is increased
Which account is affected?	FICA Tax Payable
What journal entry is made?	Credit FICA Tax Payable for $169.26

3. The $39.59 for the employer's *matching* Medicare funds becomes a liability to the business until the taxes are paid. Record the liability by crediting Medicare Tax Payable.

What is happening?	The amount of Medicare tax owed is increased
Which account is affected?	Medicare Tax Payable
What journal entry is made?	Credit Medicare Tax Payable

4. A credit of $9.88 is recorded in the Unemployment Tax Payable – Federal account to show an increase in the employer's payroll tax liability.

What is happening?	The federal unemployment tax owed is increased
Which account is affected?	Unemployment Tax Payable – Federal
What journal entry is made?	Credit Unemployment Tax Payable – Federal

5. A credit of $66.69 is recorded in the Unemployment Tax Payable – State account to show an increase in the employer's payroll tax liability.

What is happening?	The state unemployment tax owed is increased
Which account is affected?	Unemployment Tax Payable – State
What journal entry is made?	Credit Unemployment Tax Payable – State

The T accounts on the following page illustrate at a glance how these various accounts are affected. They also show the equality of the debit and credit amounts in this transaction.

Payroll Taxes Expense

Payroll Taxes Expense	
285.42	

=

FICA Tax Payable		Medicare Tax Payable		Unemployment Tax Payable – Federal		Unemployment Tax Payable – State	
	169.26		39.59		9.88		66.69

+   +   +   +

Posting Payroll Taxes

Complete the following activity.

		JOURNAL						Page 2	
Date 20—		Account Title and Explanation	Doc No.	Post. Ref.	General Debit		General Credit		
Dec.	31	Payroll Taxes Expense			285	42			
		FICA Tax Payable					169	26	
		Medicare Tax Payable					39	59	
		Unempl. Tax Pay.–Federal					9	88	
		Unempl. Tax Pay.–State	M4				66	69	

2.1   From the journal entry above, post the transactions to record the employer's payroll taxes for the pay period ending December 31 of the current year. (NOTE: The FICA and Medicare account balances as of December 15th reflect the employees' withholding *and* employer's matching funds.) The last entry to be posted was the transaction to record the December 31st payroll entry (from Section I) and represents the FICA tax withheld from the *employees'* earnings.

Account Title: FICA Tax Payable								Account No. 220	
Date 20—		Explanation	Post. Ref.	Debit		Credit		Balance Debit	Balance Credit
Dec.	15		✔						338 52
	31		J2			169 26			507 78

Account Title: *Medicare Tax Payable*   **Account No.** *230*

Date 20—		Explanation	Post. Ref.	Debit		Credit		Balance			
								Debit		Credit	
Dec.	15		✔							79	18
	31		J2			39	59			118	77

Account Title: *Unempl. Tax Payable – Federal*   **Account No.** *240*

Date 20—		Explanation	Post. Ref.	Debit		Credit		Balance			
								Debit		Credit	
Dec.	1		✔							39	52
	15		J2			9	88			49	40

Account Title: *Unempl. Tax Payable – State*   **Account No.** *250*

Date 20—		Explanation	Post. Ref.	Debit		Credit		Balance			
								Debit		Credit	
Dec.	1		✔							266	76
	15		J2			66	69			333	45

Account Title: *Payroll Taxes Expense*   **Account No.** *550*

Date 20—		Explanation	Post. Ref.	Debit		Credit		Balance			
								Debit		Credit	
Dec.	15		J2	285	42			285	42		

Review the material in this section in preparation for the Self Test. This Self Test will check your mastery of this particular section as well as your knowledge of the previous section.

SELF TEST 2

Match the following accounting terms with their definitions (each answer, 2 points).

2.01 _____ payment based on an hourly rate or a piece-work basis

a. salary

2.02 _____ a tax imposed by a state to pay benefits to the unemployed

b. wage

2.03 _____ required and voluntary amounts taken from gross earnings to determine net pay

c. employee earnings record

2.04 _____ all salaries and wages paid to employees

d. payroll register

2.05 _____ a tax used for administration of state and federal unemployment programs

e. FICA

2.06 _____ adjusts an employer's state unemployment tax liability based on a record of steady employment

f. merit rating

2.07 _____ a tax used to support social security programs

g. FUTA

2.08 _____ a period covered by a salary or wage payment

h. payroll

2.09 _____ an accounting form that summarizes payroll information for all employees during a specific pay period

i. pay period

j. payroll deductions

2.010 _____ a specified amount paid to an employee per month or per year

k. withholding allowance

2.011 _____ a form used to summarize payroll deductions and payments made to each individual employee

l. state unemployment tax

Complete the following activities (each answer, 5 points).

2.012 List the four payroll taxes employers must pay in addition to what they withhold from employees' wages.

a. _____

b. _____

c. _____

d. _____

2.013 List the four accounts involved in journalizing the monthly payment of federal payroll taxes withheld from employees' earnings.

a. _____

b. _____

c. _____

d. _____

Match the following descriptions with the correct rates or tax bases (each answer, 2 points).

2.014 _____ Medicare tax rate paid by employees

2.015 _____ FICA tax rate paid by employees

2.016 _____ FUTA maximum taxable earnings

2.017 _____ net FUTA tax rate after tax credit for employers with a state unemployment program

2.018 _____ FICA maximum taxable earnings

2.019 _____ combined Medicare tax rate for employees and employers

2.020 _____ combined FICA tax rate for employees and employers

2.021 _____ Combined FICA tax rate (Social Security and Medicare) established by Congress

a. 6.2%

b. 4.5%

c. 1.45%

d. 12.4%

e. 7.65%

f. 2.9%

g. 0.8%

h. first $7,000.00

i. first $76,200.00

SECTION III. PREPARING PAYROLL TAX REPORTS

Payment of Withholding and Payroll Taxes

At regular intervals the payroll tax liabilities must be reported and paid by employers. These liabilities are the amounts withheld from employee's earnings and the employer's payroll taxes and include: (1) FICA, Medicare and employees' federal income taxes; (2) employee's state income taxes; (3) federal and state unemployment taxes; and (4) voluntary deductions withheld from employee's earnings.

FICA, Medicare and Federal Income Taxes. The government requires *periodic payment*—usually monthly—of the following withholding taxes: (1) employee income tax withheld, (2) employees' FICA/Medicare tax, and (3) employer's FICA/Medicare tax. All three taxes are paid in a single payment. Tax payments can only be made to banks authorized by the Internal Revenue Service and must be accompanied by a Federal Tax Deposit Coupon (Form 8109, shown at right). Any Federal Reserve bank can also accept such payments.

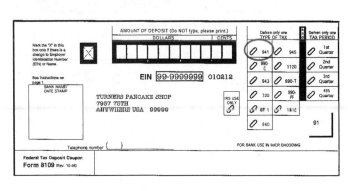

The government also requires *periodic reporting*—usually quarterly—of payroll taxes withheld. The Employer's Quarterly Federal Tax Return, Form 941 (to be discussed later in this section) is completed at the end of each quarter and shows the total federal income tax withheld and the total FICA taxes (employees' and employer's share) for the quarter. Form 941 must be filed by the last day of the month following the end of the calendar quarter. The amount of federal tax deposits that have been made (Form 8109) are listed on the return.

Whether these taxes are paid (deposited) monthly or quarterly depends upon the amount of taxes owed. The federal government requires a payment to be made when the amount of the two taxes owed (income tax and FICA/Medicare) totals more than $1,000.00 per quarter, or the employer is a required monthly depositor based on total earnings rules. Most employers are required to deposit monthly. However, based on the total earnings rules, the employer may be required to deposit taxes semimonthly or weekly.

Federal taxes are usually paid on a monthly schedule. These taxes must be deposited by the 15th of the month following the month in which they are due and payable. For example, the federal tax deposit for March must be made on or before April 15th. (In the case of the following illustrations, the deposit for the quarter ending December 31 of the current year is made on or before January 15th of the next year.)

Journalizing the Payment of Federal Payroll Taxes. The accounts that are involved in this transaction are:

1. Employee Income Tax Payable – this account contains the funds withheld from all employees' earnings for federal income tax for two pay periods in December.
2. FICA Tax Payable – this account contains both employees' funds and the employer's matching amounts.
3. Medicare Tax Payable – this account contains both employees' funds and the employer's matching amounts.
4. Cash

The journal entry to record the federal tax deposit is shown below.

Date 20—		Account Title and Explanation	Doc No.	Post. Ref.	General Debit		General Credit	
Jan.	15	Employee Income Tax Pay.			1 462	00		
		FICA Tax Payable			2 677	04		
		Medicare Tax Payable			3 158	36		
		Cash	Ck150				4 1297	40

1. The account balance of $462.00 for Employee Income Tax Payable represents income tax withheld from employee checks for the two pay periods in the month of December. This liability account has a credit balance; therefore, the account will be debited because we are decreasing the balance.

What happens?	The amount of employee income tax owed is decreased
Which account is affected?	Employee Income Tax Payable
What journal entry is made?	Debit Employee Tax Payable for $462.00

2. The $677.04 for FICA Tax Payable is the amount withheld from the employees' checks *plus* the matching funds from the employer. This liability account will be debited because we are decreasing the balance.

What happens?	The amount of FICA tax owed is decreased
Which account is affected?	FICA Tax Payable
What journal entry is made?	Debit FICA Tax Payable for $677.04

3. The $158.36 for for Medicare Tax Payable is the amount withheld from the employees' checks *plus* the employer's matching Medicare funds. This liability account will be debited because we are decreasing the balance.

What happens?	The amount of Medicare tax owed is decreased
Which account is affected?	Medicare Tax Payable
What journal entry is made?	Debit Medicare Tax Payable for $158.36

4. A credit of $1,297.40 is recorded in the Cash account to show a decrease in the account balance due to payment of these payroll taxes.

What happens?	The balance of the Cash account is decreased
Which account is affected?	Cash
What journal entry is made?	Credit Cash for $1,297.40

After the journal entry is posted, the ledger accounts for these liabilities appear as follows:

Account Title: Employee Income Tax Payable							Account No. 210	
Date 20—		Explanation	Post. Ref.	Debit		Credit	Balance	
							Debit	Credit
Jan.	1		✔					462 00
	15		J2	462 00				—

Account Title: FICA Tax Payable					Account No. 220		
Date 20—	Explanation	Post. Ref.	Debit	Credit	Balance		
					Debit	Credit	
Jan. 1		✔				677	04
15		J3	677 04			—	

Account Title: Medicare Tax Payable					Account No. 230		
Date 20—	Explanation	Post. Ref.	Debit	Credit	Balance		
					Debit	Credit	
Jan. 1		✔				158	36
15		J3	158 36			—	

Federal and State Unemployment Taxes. Normally, the federal unemployment tax is paid quarterly. It is paid using the same bank and the same coupon (Form 8109) used for the monthly income tax and FICA/Medicare tax deposits. The coupon is marked to indicate the purpose of the payment, Federal Unemployment Taxes, Form 940. The payment coupons are used quarterly; however, the Form 940 is filed at the end of the tax year. For federal tax purposes, the tax year is from January 1 to December 31.

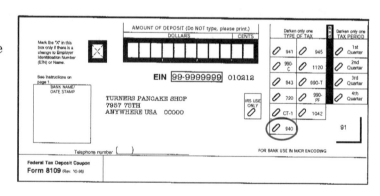

The tax deposits must be made by the last day of the month following the end of the quarter. For example, the federal unemployment tax deposit for the first quarter (January–March) must be made by April 30.

State unemployment taxes are also deposited quarterly. Tax reporting requirements and forms used will, of course, vary from state to state but state unemployment tax reports are usually filed quarterly.

Journalizing the Payment of Federal and State Unemployment Taxes. The journal entry to record the payment of the federal and state unemployment taxes discussed in Section II is shown on the following page. Both taxes are paid during the month following the end of the quarter, December 31; therefore, the journal entry is dated in January and reflects the federal and state unemployment tax liabilities for three months—October, November and December—with a semi-monthly pay period.

JOURNAL

Date 20—		Account Title and Explanation	Doc No.	Post. Ref.	General Debit		General Credit	
Jan.	15	Employee Income Tax Pay.		210	462	00		
		FICA Tax Payable		220	677	04		
		Medicare Tax Payable		230	158	36		
		Cash	Ck150	110			1297	40
	31	Unempl. Tax Pay.-Federal			59	28		
		Cash	Ck151				59	28
	31	Unempl. Tax Pay.-State			400	14		
		Cash	Ck152				400	14

After the journal entry is posted, the ledger accounts for these liabilities appear as follows:

Account Title: Unempl. Tax Payable – Federal **Account No.** 240

Date 20—		Explanation	Post. Ref.	Debit		Credit		Balance Debit		Balance Credit	
Jan.	1		✔							59	28
	15		J3			9	88			69	16
	31					9	88			79	04
	31			59	28					19	76

Account Title: Unempl. Tax Payable – State **Account No.** 250

Date 20—		Explanation	Post. Ref.	Debit		Credit		Balance Debit		Balance Credit	
Jan.	1		✔							400	14
	15		J3			66	69			466	83
	31		J3			66	69			533	52
	31		J3	400	14					133	38

Additional Payroll Liabilities

In addition to the required payroll deductions, employees may authorize voluntary deductions such as purchasing U.S. saving bonds, medical insurance, loan repayment from banks or credit unions, charitable donations, purchasing goods or services from employers and investing in savings or retirement plans.

Since voluntary deductions are withheld from the employee's paycheck, it becomes the employer's responsibility to forward these amounts to the proper agencies. This process creates additional payroll liabilities that must be maintained and accounted for by the payroll departments.

The source document for the payroll, including required and voluntary deductions, is the payroll register. The individual employee deduction record is the employee earnings record. These two documents are used to account for individual choices of deductions and the employer's liabilities.

Quarterly Payroll Tax Reports

Form 941 – Employer's Quarterly Federal Tax Return. Employers who withhold income tax on wages, or who must pay FICA/Medicare taxes, must file Form 941 each calendar quarter. The filing date is the last day for the month following the end of a calendar quarter. Total wages, tips and other compensation are listed on this form, and the total FICA/Medicare taxes are calculated using the combined percentage rate of 12.4% (6.2% contributed by the employee and 6.2% matched by the employer). The form also provides a summary of all monthly tax deposits made. Employers whose tax liability is over $1,000.00 per quarter are required to make monthly deposits at an approved bank. The summary of these deposits is listed on the bottom of the form.

An example of a completed Form 941 is shown on the following page.

Form 941 for 2010: Employer's QUARTERLY Federal Tax Return

(Rev. April 2010)

Department of the Treasury — Internal Revenue Service

951110

OMB No. 1545-0029

(EIN)
Employer identification number 1 2 – 3 4 5 6 7 8 9

Name *(not your trade name)* John J. Hart

Trade name *(if any)* Hart's Electronics

Address 1010 Anyplace Ave.
Number   Street   Suite or room number

Anytown   MS   12345
City   State   ZIP code

Report for this Quarter of 2010
(Check one.)

- [ ] **1:** January, February, March
- [ ] **2:** April, May, June
- [ ] **3:** July, August, September
- [x] **4:** October, November, December

Read the separate instructions before you complete Form 941. Type or print within the boxes.

Part 1: Answer these questions for this quarter.

1	Number of employees who received wages, tips, or other compensation for the pay period including: *Mar. 12* (Quarter 1), *June 12* (Quarter 2), *Sept. 12* (Quarter 3), or *Dec. 12* (Quarter 4) **1**	4
2	Wages, tips, and other compensation **2**	18950.00
3	Income tax withheld from wages, tips, and other compensation **3**	4610.00

4 If no wages, tips, and other compensation are subject to social security or Medicare tax
☐ Check and go to line 6e.

Report wages/tips for this quarter, including those paid to qualified new employees, on lines 5a–5c. The social security tax exemption on wages/tips will be figured on lines 6c and 6d and will reduce the tax on line 6e.

		Column 1		Column 2
5a	Taxable social security wages*	18950.00	× .124 =	2349.80
5b	Taxable social security tips*	.	× .124 =	.
5c	Taxable Medicare wages & tips*	18950.00	× .029 =	549.55

5d	Add *Column 2* line 5a, *Column 2* line 5b, and *Column 2* line 5c **5d**	2899.35

See instructions for definitions of qualified employee and exempt wages/tips.

6a	Number of qualified employees *first* paid exempt wages/tips this quarter	
6b	Number of qualified employees paid exempt wages/tips this quarter	
6c	Exempt wages/tips paid to qualified employees this quarter . × .062 = **6d**	.
6e	Total taxes before adjustments (line 3 + line 5d – line 6d = line 6e) **6e**	7509.35
7a	Current quarter's adjustment for fractions of cents **7a**	.
7b	Current quarter's adjustment for sick pay **7b**	.
7c	Current quarter's adjustments for tips and group-term life insurance **7c**	.
8	Total taxes after adjustments. Combine lines 6e through 7c **8**	7509.35
9	Advance earned income credit (EIC) payments made to employees **9**	.
10	Total taxes after adjustment for advance EIC (line 8 – line 9 = line 10) **10**	7509.35
11	Total deposits, including prior quarter overpayments **11**	7509.35
12a	COBRA premium assistance payments (see instructions) **12a**	.
12b	Number of individuals provided COBRA premium assistance	
12c	Number of qualified employees paid exempt wages/tips March 19–31	

Complete lines 12c, 12d, and 12e only for the 2nd quarter of 2010.

12d	Exempt wages/tips paid to qualified employees March 19–31 . × .062 = **12e**	.
13	Add lines 11, 12a, and 12e **13**	7509.35
14	Balance due. If line 10 is more than line 13, enter the difference and see instructions **14**	0.00
15	Overpayment. If line 13 is more than line 10, enter the difference . Check one: ☐ Apply to next return. ☐ Send a refund.	

▶ **You MUST complete both pages of Form 941 and SIGN it.**   Next ▶

For Privacy Act and Paperwork Reduction Act Notice, see the back of the Payment Voucher.   Cat. No. 17001Z   Form **941** (Rev. 4-2010)

Name *(not your trade name)*	Employer identification number (EIN)
John J. Hart	12-3456789

Part 2: Tell us about your deposit schedule and tax liability for this quarter.

If you are unsure about whether you are a monthly schedule depositor or a semiweekly schedule depositor, see *Pub. 15 (Circular E),* **section 11.**

16 [M] [S] Write the state abbreviation for the state where you made your deposits OR write "MU" if you made your deposits in *multiple* states.

17 Check one: ☐ Line 10 on this return is less than $2,500 or line 10 on the return for the preceding quarter was less than $2,500, and you did not incur a $100,000 next-day deposit obligation during the current quarter. Go to Part 3.

☐ You were a monthly schedule depositor for the entire quarter. Enter your tax liability for each month and total liability for the quarter, then go to Part 3.

Tax liability:	Month 1	2503.12
	Month 2	2503.12
	Month 3	2503.11
Total liability for quarter		7509.35	Total must equal line 10.

☐ You were a semiweekly schedule depositor for any part of this quarter. Complete *Schedule B (Form 941): Report of Tax Liability for Semiweekly Schedule Depositors,* and attach it to Form 941.

Part 3: Tell us about your business. If a question does NOT apply to your business, leave it blank.

18 If your business has closed or you stopped paying wages . . . . ☐ Check here, and

enter the final date you paid wages   [/ /] .

19 If you are a seasonal employer and you do not have to file a return for every quarter of the year . . ☐ Check here.

Part 4: May we speak with your third-party designee?

Do you want to allow an employee, a paid tax preparer, or another person to discuss this return with the IRS? See the instructions for details.

☐ Yes. Designee's name and phone number [   ] [   ]

Select a 5-digit Personal Identification Number (PIN) to use when talking to the IRS. ☐ ☐ ☐ ☐ ☐

[X] No.

Part 5: Sign here. You MUST complete both pages of Form 941 and SIGN it.

Under penalties of perjury, I declare that I have examined this return, including accompanying schedules and statements, and to the best of my knowledge and belief, it is true, correct, and complete. Declaration of preparer (other than taxpayer) is based on all information of which preparer has any knowledge.

X   **Sign your name here**   *John J. Hart*

Print your name here   John J. Hart

Print your title here   Owner

Date   1/24/20—

Best daytime phone [   ]

Paid preparer's use only	Check if you are self-employed . . . ☐
Preparer's name	Preparer's SSN/PTIN
Preparer's signature	Date / /
Firm's name (or yours if self-employed)	EIN
Address	Phone
City	State	ZIP code

Form **941** (Rev. 4-2010)

ACCOUNTING

nine

LIFEPAC TEST

93 / 116

Name _____

Date _____

Score _____

LIFEPAC TEST ACCOUNTING 9

PART I

On the blank, print a *T* if the statement is true or an *F* if the statement is false (each answer, 1 point).

1. _____ An employee's social security number must be recorded on all copies of the W-2 form.

2. _____ A W-2 form indicates the number of months an employee was employed by an employer.

3. _____ A W-2 form reports only the net pay received by an employee for the entire year.

4. _____ If an employee is employed by several businesses during the year, each employer must furnish the employee with a W-2 statement.

5. _____ Form W-3 is used by an employee to inform his employer of all withholding allowances.

6. _____ A Form W-2 shows the total FICA tax withheld from an employee's wages.

7. _____ The federal government collects Medicare tax on all wages and compensation earned by an employee.

8. _____ The federal government Form 940 is used to report federal unemployment taxes.

9. _____ Under current federal regulations, each employee has a maximum tax base upon which FICA taxes are paid.

10. _____ An employer is required to provide each employee with a W-2 Form no later than April 15 of the current tax year.

11. _____ The form that is sent by an employer to the Social Security Administration that summarizes total earnings and withholding of all employees is the W-3 Form.

12. _____ The major purpose of the Federal Unemployment Insurance Act is to provide financial assistance to each state to develop a state unemployment insurance program.

13. _____ Each employer must file a Form 941 quarterly to report total earnings and withholding for that calendar quarter.

14. _____ The payroll register is used as a source of information to complete an employee's W-2 form.

15. _____ Congress is responsible for setting the tax base and tax rate for FICA taxes.

For each statement below, circle the letter of the choice that best completes the sentence (each answer, 1 point).

16. The source of information to record the payroll entry is:
    a. check register
    b. employees earnings record
    c. payroll register
    d. work sheet

17. Employers report quarterly federal tax withheld on Form:
    a. 940
    b. 941
    c. W-2
    d. W-4

18. Payroll systems used by businesses:
    a. are designed by the federal government
    b. are designed by the state government
    c. are designed by the business
    d. are designed by the labor union

19. A payroll tax that cannot be deducted from an employee's wages is:
    a. federal income tax
    b. federal unemployment tax
    c. state income tax
    d. FICA tax

20. After the end of each calendar year, the employer must provide each employee with:
    a. a W-2 Form
    b. Form 1099
    c. Form 941
    d. a W-4 form

21. When a payroll is paid, the credit to Cash is equal to the:
    a. net pay of all employees
    b. total earnings of all employees
    c. total payroll deductions
    d. total FICA and Medicare taxes

22. FICA taxes and Medicare taxes withheld from employees' wages should be posted to:
    a. an asset account
    b. a liability account
    c. an expense account
    d. a revenue account

23. Medicare taxes are paid:
    a. by employers only
    b. equally by both employer and employee
    c. by employees only
    d. none of these

24. The amount an employee receives after deductions is referred to as:
    a. regular earnings
    b. overtime wages
    c. net pay
    d. total earnings

25. The employer's payroll taxes are posted to the:
    a. general journal
    b. payroll register
    c. any journal
    d. general ledger accounts

26. The amount of total earnings for a pay period is posted to:
    a. a revenue account
    b. an asset account
    c. a liability account
    d. an expense account

27. Any withholding from an employee's wages is classified as a/an:
    a. asset
    b. owner's equity
    c. liability
    d. expense

28. The employer's payroll taxes are posted to a/an:
    a. expense account
    b. asset account
    c. liability account
    d. revenue account

2

29. A separate general ledger account for each employee is replaced by
    a. a journal and check register
    b. the payroll register and employee earnings record
    c. an expense and a liability
    d. the payroll check and a payroll check

30. The factor that reduces the employer's liability for state unemployment tax is called:
    a. a tax incentive
    b. a tax liability factor
    c. an employer merit rating
    d. a payment to the federal unemployment insurance program.

31. The federal income tax column of the payroll register is posted to:
    a. an expense account   b. an asset account
    c. a revenue account   d. a liability account

32. To record the employer's payroll taxes expense, the following accounts are credited:
    a. Medicare Tax Payable, Unemployment Tax Payable–State and Unemployment Tax Payable–Federal
    b. FICA Tax Payable, Medicare Tax Payable, Unemployment Tax Payable–Federal and Unemployment Tax Payable–State
    c. Employee Income Tax Payable, FICA Tax Payable, Medicare Tax Payable and Unemployment Tax Payable–Federal
    d. Employee Income Tax Payable, United Way Payable, Medicare Tax Payable and FICA Tax Payable

33. A payroll register is completed at the end of each:
    a. pay period   b. month
    c. year   d. week

34. A semimonthly payroll contains:
    a. 52 pay periods   b. 12 pay periods
    c. 24 pay periods   d. 13 pay periods

35. Federal and state unemployment taxes are to be paid by the:
    a. government   b. employee
    c. employee and employer equally d. employer

36. FICA taxes are to be paid by the:
    a. government   b. employee
    c. employee and employer equally d. employer

37. The required deductions from an employee's wages are:
    a. federal and state income taxes, FICA taxes and medicare taxes
    b. federal and state unemployment taxes, FICA taxes, and federal and state employee income taxes
    c. U.S. Savings Bonds, United Way contributions, and federal and state income taxes
    d. federal and state income taxes, U.S. Savings Bonds, United Way contributions and union dues

38. The maximum earnings tax base for federal and state unemployment taxes is:
    a. $8,600.00   b. $6,500.00
    c. $7,000.00   d. $9,500.00.

39. Medical and hospitalization insurance is an example of a:
   a. required deduction
   b. a voluntary deduction
   c. federal deduction
   d. state deduction

40. One major purpose of any state unemployment insurance program is to:
   a. assist employers with payroll taxes
   b. pay the federal government unemployment insurance
   c. pay benefits to unemployed individuals
   d. assist employers in meeting payroll costs

Match the following accounting terms with their definitions (each answer, 1 point).

41. _____ payment based on an hourly rate or a piece-work basis

42. _____ a tax imposed by a state to pay benefits to the unemployed

43. _____ required and voluntary amounts taken from gross earnings to determine net pay

44. _____ all salaries and wages paid to employees

45. _____ a tax used for administration of state and federal unemployment programs

46. _____ adjusts an employer's state unemployment tax liability based on a record of steady employment

47. _____ a tax used to support social security programs

48. _____ a period covered by a salary or wage payment

49. _____ an accounting form that summarizes payroll information for all employees during a specific pay period

50. _____ a specified amount paid to an employee per month or per year

51. _____ a form used to summarize payroll deductions and payments made to each individual employee

a. employee earnings record

b. FICA

c. FUTA

d. merit rating

e. pay period

f. payroll

g. payroll deductions

h. payroll register

i. salary

j. state unemployment tax

k. wage

l. withholding allowance

4

PART II

Journalize the payroll entries (65 points total).

The totals of CyberVision's payroll registers for the month March of the current year are shown below. Payroll tax rates are as follows: FICA, 6.2%; Medicare, 1.45%; federal unemployment, 0.8%; state unemployment, 5.4%. No employees have reached the maximum tax base.

Instructions:

1. Journalize the March 15th payroll, Ck260. The journal page number is 3.

2. Calculate and record the employer's payroll taxes for the March 15th payroll, M4.†

3. Journalize the March 31st payroll, Ck290.

4. Calculate and record the employer's payroll taxes for the March 31st payroll, M7.†

† Use the form provided on page 7 of this LIFEPAC Test.

March Payroll Register totals:

Pay Period	Total Earnings	Federal Income Tax	FICA Tax	Medicare Tax	Other*	Total Deductions	Net Pay
Mar. 1–15	$6,270.00	$694.00	$388.74	$ 90.92	(S)$100.00	$1,273.66	$4,996.34
Mar. 16–31	$6,982.00	$797.00	$432.88	$101.24	(S)$ 75.00	$1,406.12	$5,575.88

*Other: (S) = U.S. Savings Bonds

JOURNAL

Page

Date		Account Title and Explanation	Doc No.	Post. Ref.	General Debit		General Credit	

Payroll Tax Summary Sheet March 15, 20–   *Memo #4*

	Debit	*Credit*
Payroll Taxes Expense	_____	
FICA Tax Payable		_____
Medicare Tax Payable		_____
Unemployment Tax Payable – Federal		_____
Unemployment Tax Payable – State		_____

Payroll Tax Summary Sheet March 31, 20–   *Memo #7*

	Debit	*Credit*
Payroll Taxes Expense	_____	
FICA Tax Payable		_____
Medicare Tax Payable		_____
Unemployment Tax Payable – Federal		_____
Unemployment Tax Payable – State		_____

Annual Payroll Tax Reports

Form W-2 – Wage and Tax Statement. Each employer who withholds federal income tax and FICA/Medicare taxes from employees must provide an annual report of the withholdings. Each employee must receive from the employer a W-2 statement showing total earnings and the amounts withheld for taxes from the employee's earnings. The source of information to complete this form is the employee earnings record.

Each employee must receive a Form W-2 by January 31 of the next year. A sample of a completed W-2 is shown below.

a Employee's social security number				

Employee's social security number: 123-45-6789

OMB No. 1545-0008

Safe, accurate, FAST! Use IRS e-file

Visit the IRS website at www.irs.gov/efile.

b Employer identification number (EIN): 12-3456789

1 Wages, tips, other compensation: 22910.00
2 Federal income tax withheld: 4582.00

c Employer's name, address, and ZIP code:
Hart's Electronics
1010 Anyplace Ave.
Anytown, MS 12345

3 Social security wages: 22910.00
4 Social security tax withheld: 1420.42

5 Medicare wages and tips: 22910.00
6 Medicare tax withheld: 332.20

7 Social security tips
8 Allocated tips

d Control number

9 Advance EIC payment
10 Dependent care benefits

e Employee's first name and initial — Last name — Suff.:
Andrea C. Baker
1341 Louisa Street
Anytown, MS 12345

11 Nonqualified plans
12a See instructions for box 12

13 Statutory employee / Retirement plan / Third-party sick pay
12b

14 Other
12c

12d

f Employee's address and ZIP code

15 State: MS — Employer's state ID number: 20-12345
16 State wages, tips, etc.: 22910.00
17 State income tax: 2520.10
18 Local wages, tips, etc.
19 Local income tax
20 Locality name

Form **W-2** Wage and Tax Statement

2009

Department of the Treasury—Internal Revenue Service

Copy B—To Be Filed With Employee's FEDERAL Tax Return.
This information is being furnished to the Internal Revenue Service.

Form W-3 – Transmittal of Income and Tax Statements. Each employer must submit Form W-3 (Transmittal of Income and Tax Statements) to the Social Security Administration. This form reports the previous year's earnings and payroll taxes withheld. Form W-3 must be submitted by February 28, along with Copy A of each employee's W-2 form.

As example of a completed Form W-3 is shown on the next page.

a Control number	**33333**	For Official Use Only ▶ OMB No. 1545-0008		

b Kind of Payer	941 ☒ Military ☐ 943 ☐ 944 ☐ CT-1 ☐ Hshld. emp. ☐ Medicare govt. emp. ☐ Third-party sick pay ☐	**1** Wages, tips, other compensation	**2** Federal income tax withheld
		3 Social security wages 66900.00	**4** Social security tax withheld 18732.00
c Total number of Forms W-2 **4**	**d** Establishment number	**5** Medicare wages and tips 66900.00	**6** Medicare tax withheld 4147.80
e Employer identification number (EIN) 12-3456789		**7** Social security tips 66900.00	**8** Allocated tips 970.05
f Employer's name *Hart's Electronics*		**9** Advance EIC payments	**10** Dependent care benefits
1010 Anyplace Ave.		**11** Nonqualified plans	**12** Deferred compensation
Anytown, MS 12345		**13** For third-party sick pay use only	
		14 Income tax withheld by payer of third-party sick pay	
g Employer's address and ZIP code			
h Other EIN used this year			

15 State Employer's state ID number	**16** State wages, tips, etc.	**17** State income tax
	18 Local wages, tips, etc.	**19** Local income tax

Contact person *John J. Hart*	Telephone number ( )	For Official Use Only
Email address	Fax number ( )	

Under penalties of perjury, I declare that I have examined this return and accompanying documents, and, to the best of my knowledge and belief, they are true, correct, and complete.

Signature ▶ *John J. Hart* Title ▶ *Owner* Date ▶ *1-24-20—*

Form **W-3** Transmittal of Wage and Tax Statements   **2009**   Department of the Treasury
Internal Revenue Service

Send this entire page with the entire Copy A page of Form(s) W-2 to the Social Security Administration.

Do not send any payment (cash, checks, money orders, etc.) with Forms W-2 and W-3.

Reminder

Separate instructions. See the 2009 Instructions for Forms W-2 and W-3 for information on completing this form.

Purpose of Form

A Form W-3 Transmittal is completed only when paper Copy A of Form(s) W-2, Wage and Tax Statement, are being filed. Do not file Form W-3 alone. Do not file Form W-3 for Form(s) W-2 that were submitted electronically to the Social Security Administration (see below). All paper forms **must** comply with IRS standards and be machine readable. Photocopies and hand-printed forms are **not** acceptable. Use a Form W-3 even if only one paper Form W-2 is being filed. Make sure both the Form W-3 and Form(s) W-2 show the correct tax year and Employer Identification Number (EIN). Make a copy of this form and keep it with Copy D (For Employer) of Form(s) W-2 for your records.

Electronic Filing

The Social Security Administration strongly suggests employers report Form W-3 and W-2 Copy A electronically instead of on paper. SSA provides two e-file options:

● Free online, fill-in Forms W-2 for employers who file 20 or fewer Form(s) W-2.

● Upload a file for employers who use payroll/tax software to print Form(s) W-2, if the vendor software creates a file that can be uploaded to SSA.

For more information, go to *www.socialsecurity.gov/employer* and select "First Time Filers" or "Returning Filers" under "BEFORE YOU FILE."

When To File

Mail any paper Forms W-2 under cover of this Form W-3 Transmittal by March 1, 2010. Electronic fill-in forms or uploads are filed through SSA's Business Services Online (BSO) Internet site and will be on time if submitted by March 31, 2010.

Where To File Paper Forms

Send this entire page with the entire Copy A page of Form(s) W-2 to:

**Social Security Administration
Data Operations Center
Wilkes-Barre, PA 18769-0001**

Note. If you use "Certified Mail" to file, change the ZIP code to "18769-0002." If you use an IRS-approved private delivery service, add "ATTN: W-2 Process, 1150 E. Mountain Dr." to the address and change the ZIP code to "18702-7997." See Publication 15 (Circular E), Employer's Tax Guide, for a list of IRS-approved private delivery services.

For Privacy Act and Paperwork Reduction Act Notice, see the back of Copy D of Form W-2.
Cat. No. 10159Y

Form 940 – Employer's Annual Federal Unemployment (FUTA) Tax Return. An employer must file an annual return Form 94 by January 31 of the following year to report the total federal and state unemployment taxes paid during the previous year. A completed Form 940 is shown below:

NOTE: The tax form, as well as income and tax amounts are for sample purposes. The amounts may not reflect what the student is familiar with.

Form **940 for 2009:** Employer's Annual Federal Unemployment (FUTA) Tax Return   850109

Department of the Treasury — Internal Revenue Service

OMB No. 1545-0028

(EIN)
Employer identification number   `1 2 - 3 4 5 6 7 8 9`

Name (not your trade name)   John J. Hart

Trade name (if any)   Hart's Electronics

Address   1010 Anyplace Ave.
Number   Street   Suite or room number

Anytown   MS   12345
City   State   ZIP code

Type of Return
(Check all that apply.)

- [ ] a. Amended
- [ ] b. Successor employer
- [ ] c. No payments to employees in 2009
- [ ] d. Final: Business closed or stopped paying wages

Read the separate instructions before you fill out this form. Please type or print within the boxes.

Part 1: Tell us about your return. If any line does NOT apply, leave it blank.

1   If you were required to pay your state unemployment tax in ...

    1a One state only, write the state abbreviation . . . . . 1a `M S`

    - OR -

    1b More than one state (You are a multi-state employer) . . . . 1b [ ] Check here. Fill out Schedule A.

2   If you paid wages in a state that is subject to CREDIT REDUCTION . . . . 2 [ ] Check here. Fill out Schedule A. (Form 940), Part 2.

Part 2: Determine your FUTA tax before adjustments for 2009. If any line does NOT apply, leave it blank.

3   Total payments to all employees 3   66900.00

4   Payments exempt from FUTA tax 4   .

    Check all that apply: 4a [ ] Fringe benefits   4c [ ] Retirement/Pension   4e [ ] Other
    4b [ ] Group-term life insurance   4d [ ] Dependent care

5   Total of payments made to each employee in excess of $7,000 5   42000.00

6   Subtotal (line 4 + line 5 = line 6) 6   .

7   Total taxable FUTA wages (line 3 – line 6 = line 7) 7   42000.00

8   FUTA tax before adjustments (line 7 × .008 = line 8) 8   24900.00

Part 3: Determine your adjustments. If any line does NOT apply, leave it blank.

9   If ALL of the taxable FUTA wages you paid were excluded from state unemployment tax, multiply line 7 by .054 (line 7 × .054 = line 9). Then go to line 12 9   .

10   If SOME of the taxable FUTA wages you paid were excluded from state unemployment tax, OR you paid ANY state unemployment tax late (after the due date for filing Form 940), fill out the worksheet in the instructions. Enter the amount from line 7 of the worksheet 10   .

11   If credit reduction applies, enter the amount from line 3 of Schedule A (Form 940) 11   .

Part 4: Determine your FUTA tax and balance due or overpayment for 2009. If any line does NOT apply, leave it blank.

12   Total FUTA tax after adjustments (lines 8 + 9 + 10 + 11 = line 12) 12   199.20

13   FUTA tax deposited for the year, including any overpayment applied from a prior year . . 13   199.20

14   Balance due (If line 12 is more than line 13, enter the difference on line 14.)
    ● If line 14 is more than $500, you must deposit your tax.
    ● If line 14 is $500 or less, you may pay with this return. For more information on how to pay, see the separate instructions 14   0.00

15   Overpayment (If line 13 is more than line 12, enter the difference on line 15 and check a box below.) 15   .

Check one: [ ] Apply to next return.
    [ ] Send a refund.

▶ You **MUST** fill out both pages of this form and **SIGN** it.

Next ➡

For Privacy Act and Paperwork Reduction Act Notice, see the back of Form 940-V, Payment Voucher.   Cat. No. 11234O   Form **940** (2009)

850209

Name *(not your trade name)*
John J. Hart

Employer identification number (EIN)
12-3456789

Part 5: Report your FUTA tax liability by quarter only if line 12 is more than $500. If not, go to Part 6.

16 Report the amount of your FUTA tax liability for each quarter; do NOT enter the amount you deposited. If you had no liability for a quarter, leave the line blank.

16a 1st quarter (January 1 – March 31) **16a**	66.40
16b 2nd quarter (April 1 – June 30) **16b**	66.40
16c 3rd quarter (July 1 – September 30) **16c**	66.40
16d 4th quarter (October 1 – December 31) **16d**	0.00

17 **Total tax liability for the year** (lines 16a + 16b + 16c + 16d = line 17) **17**   199.20   **Total must equal line 12.**

Part 6: May we speak with your third-party designee?

Do you want to allow an employee, a paid tax preparer, or another person to discuss this return with the IRS? See the instructions for details.

☐ **Yes.** Designee's name and phone number   (   )   –

Select a 5-digit Personal Identification Number (PIN) to use when talking to IRS ☐ ☐ ☐ ☐ ☐

☒ **No.**

Part 7: Sign here. You MUST fill out both pages of this form and SIGN it.

Under penalties of perjury, I declare that I have examined this return, including accompanying schedules and statements, and to the best of my knowledge and belief, it is true, correct, and complete, and that no part of any payment made to a state unemployment fund claimed as a credit was, or is to be, deducted from the payments made to employees. Declaration of preparer (other than taxpayer) is based on all information of which preparer has any knowledge.

X Sign your name here   John J. Hart

Print your name here   John J. Hart

Print your title here   Owner

Date   1 24 20

Best daytime phone   (333) 222-6789

Paid preparer's use only

Check if you are self-employed . . . ☐

Preparer's name		Preparer's SSN/PTIN
Preparer's signature		Date / /
Firm's name (or yours if self-employed)		EIN
Address		Phone ( ) –
City	State	ZIP code

Form **940** (2009)

Complete the following activity.

3.1 From the list of payroll taxes below, determine whether the employee, employer, or both are responsible for paying the tax. Place a check mark in the proper column(s).

Payroll Tax	Employee	Employer
Federal Income Taxes		
State Unemployment Taxes		
FICA (Social Security) Taxes		
Federal Unemployment Taxes		
State Income Taxes		
Medicare Taxes		

3.2 Determine the amount of earnings that are subject to state and federal unemployment taxes. Remember, unemployment taxes are owed on the first $7,000.00 of earnings for each employee.

Employee	Accumulated Earnings 10/31/20–	Total Earnings on 11/15/20–	Unemployment Taxable Earnings
Abelman, Adam	$10,200.00	$800.00	a.
Cain, Evelyn	6,400.00	800.00	b.
Isaacs, Jacob	2,890.00	350.00	c.
Jericho, Joshua	6,690.00	695.00	d.
Solomon, David	6,840.00	185.00	e.

TOTALS: f. _____   g. _____   h. _____

3.3 Use the appropriate column totals above to calculate the following payroll taxes:

a. FICA Tax Payable (6.2%) $ _____

b. Medicare Tax Payable (1.45%) $ _____

c. Federal Unemployment Tax Payable (0.8%) $ _____

d. State Unemployment Tax Payable (5.4%) $ _____

Review the material in this section in preparation for the Self Test. This Self Test will check your mastery of this particular section as well as your knowledge of the previous sections.

SELF TEST 3

For each statement below, circle the letter of the choice that best completes the sentence (each answer, 2 points).

3.01 Form 941 is filed:
    a. semimonthly   b. monthly
    c. quarterly   d. annually

3.02 Form 940 is filed:
    a. semimonthly   b. monthly
    c. quarterly   d. annually

3.03 Federal unemployment taxes are usually paid:
    a. semimonthly   b. monthly
    c. quarterly   d. annually

3.04 Form W-3 is filed:
    a. semimonthly   b. monthly
    c. quarterly   d. annually

3.05 Form W-2 is distributed to employees:
    a. semimonthly   b. monthly
    c. quarterly   d. annually

3.06 State unemployment taxes are usually paid:
    a. semimonthly   b. monthly
    c. quarterly   d. annually

3.07 Employee income taxes withheld are usually paid:
    a. semimonthly   b. monthly
    c. quarterly   d. annually

3.08 State unemployment tax forms are usually filed:
    a. semimonthly   b. monthly
    c. quarterly   d. annually

3.09 FICA taxes are paid:
    a. semimonthly   b. monthly
    c. quarterly   d. annually

3.010 Medicare taxes are paid:
    a. semimonthly   b. monthly
    c. quarterly   d. annually

3.011 The form used to make monthly federal tax deposits is:
    a. Form 941   b. Form 8109
    c. Form W-4   d. Form 1040

3.012 The form given to employees that lists their total wages and withholding for the year is:
    a. Form 1040   b. Form W-2
    c. Form W-3   d. Form W-4

3.013 The form the employer sends to the Social Security Administration showing total wages and withholding amounts for employees is called:

    a. Form 940   b. Form W-3

    c. Form W-4   d. Form 8109

3.014 Federal unemployment tax is paid:

    a. on the first $76,200.00 of an employee's earnings

    b. on the last $7,000.00 of an employee's earnings

    c. on the first $6,000.00 of an employee's earnings

    d. on the first $7,000.00 of an employee's earnings

3.015 Payroll taxes are journalized:

    a. at the end of the year   b. at the end of the payroll period

    c. at the end of the month   d. on the last day of the quarter

3.016 The employer matches employee withholding amounts for:

    a. state unemployment taxes

    b. FICA/Medicare taxes

    c. federal nuisance taxes

    d. state income tax

3.017 An employer's merit rating is based upon:

    a. the number of people he employs

    b. the number of employees hired during busy season

    c. the number of satisfied employees he has

    d. the number of employees laid off during slack seasons

3.018 The FUTA tax is based upon:

    a. the employer's merit rating   b. employees' accumulated earnings

    c. employees' net earnings   d. the total amount of income tax withheld

3.019 List the four payroll taxes employers must pay in addition to what they withhold from the employees' wages (each answer, 5 points).

    a. _____

    b. _____

    c. _____

    d. _____

3.020 List the four accounts involved in journalizing the monthly payment of federal payroll taxes withheld from employees' earnings (each answer, 5 points).

    a. _____

    b. _____

    c. _____

    d. _____

SECTION IV. REVIEW & APPLICATION PROBLEMS

Journalizing and Posting Semimonthly Payrolls

CyberVision is a technology company with a semimonthly payroll period. The totals of the payroll registers for the two pay periods in January (January 15 and January 31 of the current year) are shown below:

Pay Period	Total Earnings	Federal Income Tax	FICA Tax	Medicare Tax	Other*	Total Deductions	Net Pay
Jan. 1–15	$5,827.00	$684.00	$361.27	$84.49	(U)$150.00	$1,279.76	$4,547.24
Jan. 16–31	$4,982.00	$597.00	$308.88	$72.24	(U) $95.00	$1,073.12	$3,908.88

*Other: (U) = United Way Contributions

 Complete the following activities.

Instructions:

Notes: The general ledger accounts have already been opened. The Cash account is not complete—it reflects only the current payroll transactions. This account is provided for posting purposes only.

4.1   a. Journalize the January 15th payroll. Use page 1 of the journal. Ck #286 was issued to the payroll account.

   b. Use the Payroll Tax Summary Sheet (page 36) to calculate and record the employer's payroll taxes for the January 15th payroll (FICA, 6.2%; Medicare, 1.45%; federal unemployment, 0.8%; state unemployment, 5.4%), M3. (NOTE: No employees have yet exceeded the maximum taxable wages for calculating unemployment taxes.)

   c. Post all January 15th payroll entries.

d. Journalize the January 31st payroll. Ck #359 was issued to the payroll account.

e. Calculate and record the employer's payroll taxes for the January 31st payroll, M6.

f. Post all January 31st payroll entries.

JOURNAL					Page	
Date	Account Title and Explanation	Doc No.	Post. Ref.	General Debit		General Credit	

Payroll Tax Summary Sheet January 15, 20–   *Memo #3*

	Debit	*Credit*
Payroll Taxes Expense	_____	
FICA Tax Payable		_____
Medicare Tax Payable		_____
Unemployment Tax Payable – Federal		_____
Unemployment Tax Payable – State		_____

Payroll Tax Summary Sheet January 31, 20–   *Memo #6*

	Debit	*Credit*
Payroll Taxes Expense	_____	
FICA Tax Payable		_____
Medicare Tax Payable		_____
Unemployment Tax Payable – Federal		_____
Unemployment Tax Payable – State		_____

Account Title: *Cash*   **Account No.** *110*

Date 20–		Explanation	Post. Ref.	Debit		Credit		Balance			
								Debit		Credit	
Jan.	1		✔					10980	00		

Account Title: Employee Income Tax Payable   Account No. 210

Date 20—	Explanation	Post. Ref.	Debit	Credit	Balance Debit	Credit

Account Title: FICA Tax Payable   Account No. 220

Date 20—	Explanation	Post. Ref.	Debit	Credit	Balance Debit	Credit

Account Title: Medicare Tax Payable   Account No. 230

Date 20—	Explanation	Post. Ref.	Debit	Credit	Balance Debit	Credit

Account Title: Unempl. Tax Payable – Federal   Account No. 240

Date 20—	Explanation	Post. Ref.	Debit	Credit	Balance Debit	Credit

Account Title: Unempl. Tax Payable – State   Account No. 250

Date 20—	Explanation	Post. Ref.	Debit	Credit	Balance Debit	Balance Credit

Account Title: United Way Payable   Account No. 270

Date 20—	Explanation	Post. Ref.	Debit	Credit	Balance Debit	Balance Credit

Account Title: Payroll Taxes Expense   Account No. 550

Date 20—	Explanation	Post. Ref.	Debit	Credit	Balance Debit	Balance Credit

Account Title: Salary Expense   Account No. 570

Date 20—	Explanation	Post. Ref.	Debit	Credit	Balance Debit	Balance Credit

Paying Payroll Taxes

Lazy River Campground has a semimonthly payroll period. The company's employees make regular contributions to United Way. The company forwards these contributions at the end of each month for the previous month. The totals of the payroll registers for the two pay periods in July (July 15 and July 31 of the current year) are shown on the following page.

 Complete the following activities.

Instructions:

Notes: The general ledger accounts have already been opened and show balances as of July 1 of the current year. The Cash account is not complete—it reflects only the current payroll transactions. This account is provided for posting purpose only.

4.2 **Transactions for July 15 of the current year:**

    a. Record and post payment of the June liability for employee income tax, FICA tax and Medicare tax, Ck148. Use page 4 of the journal.

    b. Record the July 15th payroll, Ck149.

    c. Use the Payroll Tax Summary Sheet to calculate and record the employer's payroll taxes for the July 15th payroll (FICA, 6.2%; Medicare, 1.45%; federal unemployment, 0.8%; state unemployment, 5.4%), M4. (NOTE: No employees have yet exceeded the maximum taxable wages for calculating unemployment taxes.)

    d. Post all July 15th payroll entries.

Transactions for July 31 of the current year:

e. Record and post payment of the federal unemployment taxes for the quarter ended June 30, Ck150.

f. Record and post payment of the state unemployment taxes for the quarter ended June 30, Ck151.

g. Record and post payment of the employee United Way contributions from June, Ck152.

h. Record the July 31 payroll, Ck153.

i. Use the Payroll Tax Summary Sheet to calculate and record the employer's payroll taxes for the July 31 payroll, M8.

j. Post all July 31st payroll entries.

Pay Period	Total Earnings	Federal Income Tax	FICA Tax	Medicare Tax	Other*	Total Deductions	Net Pay
July 1–15	$3,212.00	$489.00	$199.14	$46.57	(U)$128.48	$863.19	$2,348.81
July 16–30	$3,180.00	$439.00	$197.16	$46.11	(U)$100.00	$782.27	$2,397.73

*Other: (U) = United Way Contributions

Payroll Tax Summary Sheet July 15, 20–   *Memo #4*

	Debit	Credit
Payroll Taxes Expense	_____	
FICA Tax Payable		_____
Medicare Tax Payable		_____
Unemployment Tax Payable – Federal		_____
Unemployment Tax Payable – State		_____

Payroll Tax Summary Sheet July 31, 20–   *Memo #8*

	Debit	Credit
Payroll Taxes Expense	_____	
FICA Tax Payable		_____
Medicare Tax Payable		_____
Unemployment Tax Payable – Federal		_____
Unemployment Tax Payable – State		_____

JOURNAL

Date	Account Title and Explanation	Doc No.	Post. Ref.	General Debit		General Credit	

NOTE: *This page may be removed from the LIFEPAC for ease in journalizing and posting these transactions.*

Extra Form:

	JOURNAL						Page	
Date	Account Title and Explanation	Doc No.	Post. Ref.	General Debit		General Credit		

Account Title: Cash   **Account No.** 110

Date 20—		Explanation	Post. Ref.	Debit		Credit		Balance			
								Debit		Credit	
July	1		✔					15890	25		

Account Title: Employee Income Tax Payable   **Account No.** 210

Date 20—		Explanation	Post. Ref.	Debit		Credit		Balance			
								Debit		Credit	
July	1		✔							896	00

Account Title: FICA Tax Payable   **Account No.** 220

Date 20—		Explanation	Post. Ref.	Debit		Credit		Balance			
								Debit		Credit	
July	1		✔							376	84

Account Title: Medicare Tax Payable — Account No. 230

Date 20—		Explanation	Post. Ref.	Debit		Credit		Balance Debit		Credit	
July	1		✔							88	13

Account Title: Unempl. Tax Payable – Federal — Account No. 240

Date 20—		Explanation	Post. Ref.	Debit		Credit		Balance Debit		Credit	
July	1		✔							159	84

Account Title: Unempl. Tax Payable – State — Account No. 250

Date 20—		Explanation	Post. Ref.	Debit		Credit		Balance Debit		Credit	
July	1		✔							887	92

Account Title: United Way Payable   Account No. 260

Date 20—	Explanation	Post. Ref.	Debit	Credit	Balance Debit	Balance Credit
July 1		✔				299 20

Account Title: Payroll Taxes Expense   Account No. 550

Date 20—	Explanation	Post. Ref.	Debit	Credit	Balance Debit	Balance Credit

Account Title: Salary Expense   Account No. 570

Date 20—	Explanation	Post. Ref.	Debit	Credit	Balance Debit	Balance Credit

Mastering Payroll Transactions

Hart Electronics completed the following payroll transactions for the months of September and October of the current year. The company has a semimonthly pay period. Payroll tax rates are as follows: FICA, 6.2%; Medicare, 1.45%; federal unemployment, 0.8%; state unemployment, 5.4%. The company buys savings bonds for employees as their accumulated withholding permits. Many of the employees also contribute to the United Way. Contributions are forwarded to the proper agency by the employer. No total earnings have exceeded the maximum tax base limit.

The balances appear in the general ledger as of Sept. 1. The Cash account is not complete—it reflects only the current payroll transactions—nor are the expense accounts closed out at the end of the month. These accounts are provided for posting purposes only.

Instructions:

Complete each part of this activity in the following order:

1. Journalize and post the transactions for September 15th. Begin with page 8 of the journal.

2. Journalize and post the transactions for September 30th.

3. Journalize and post the transactions for October 15th.

4. Journalize and post the transactions for October 31st.

NOTE: *This page may be removed from the LIFEPAC for ease in journalizing and posting these transactions.*

September Payroll Register totals:

Pay Period	Total Earnings	Federal Income Tax	FICA Tax	Medicare Tax	Other*	Total Deductions	Net Pay
Sept. 1–15	$6,548.39	$982.00	$406.00	$94.95	(S)$126.00 (U)$ 88.50	$1,697.45	$4,850.94
Sept. 16–30	$6,607.41	$997.00	$409.66	$95.81	(S)$100.00 (U)$ 81.00	$1,683.47	$4,923.94

*Other: (U) = United Way Contributions   (S) = Savings Bonds

Sept. 15 Paid previous month's liabilities for employee income tax, $1,959.00; FICA tax, $1,599.60; and Medicare tax, $347.55, Ck678.

15 Paid cash for semimonthly payroll, $4,850.94, Ck679.

15 Use the Payroll Tax Summary Sheet on the following page to calculate and record the employer payroll taxes expense, M8.

15 Paid cash for U.S. Savings Bonds, $350.00, Ck680.

15 Paid cash for employees United Way contributions, $114.00, Ck681.

30 Paid cash for semimonthly payroll, $4,923.94, Ck682.

30 Use the Payroll Tax Summary Sheet on the following page to calculate and record the employer payroll taxes expense, M9.

October Payroll Register totals:

Pay Period	Total Earnings	Federal Income Tax	FICA Tax	Medicare Tax	Other*	Total Deductions	Net Pay
Oct. 1–15	$6,710.00	$1,082.00	$416.02	$97.30	(S) $75.00 (U) $85.00	$1,755.32	$4,954.68
Oct. 16–31	$6,440.00	$897.00	$399.28	$93.38	(S)$150.00 (U)$ 65.00	$1,604.66	$4,835.34

*Other: (U) = United Way Contributions   (S) = Savings Bonds

Oct. 15 Paid previous month's liabilities for employee income tax, $1,979.00; FICA tax, $1,631.32; and Medicare tax, $381.52, Ck683.

15 Paid cash for semimonthly payroll, $4,954.68, Ck684.

15 Use the Payroll Tax Summary Sheet on the following page to calculate and record the employer payroll taxes expense, M10.

15 Paid cash for U.S. Savings Bonds, $226.00, Ck685.

15 Paid cash for employees' United Way contributions, $169.50, Ck686.

31 Paid cash for semimonthly payroll, $4,835.34, Ck687.

31 Use the Payroll Tax Summary Sheet on the following page to calculate and record the employer payroll taxes expense, M11.

31 Paid cash for federal unemployment tax for the quarter ended Sept. 30, Ck688.

31 Paid cash for state unemployment tax for the quarter ended Sept. 30, Ck689.

49

Payroll Tax Summary Sheet September 15, 20–   *Memo #8*

	Debit	*Credit*
Payroll Taxes Expense	_____	
FICA Tax Payable		_____
Medicare Tax Payable		_____
Unemployment Tax Payable – Federal		_____
Unemployment Tax Payable – State		_____

Payroll Tax Summary Sheet September 30, 20–   *Memo #9*

	Debit	*Credit*
Payroll Taxes Expense	_____	
FICA Tax Payable		_____
Medicare Tax Payable		_____
Unemployment Tax Payable – Federal		_____
Unemployment Tax Payable – State		_____

Payroll Tax Summary Sheet October 15, 20–   *Memo #10*

	Debit	*Credit*
Payroll Taxes Expense	_____	
FICA Tax Payable		_____
Medicare Tax Payable		_____
Unemployment Tax Payable – Federal		_____
Unemployment Tax Payable – State		_____

Payroll Tax Summary Sheet October 31, 20–   *Memo #11*

	Debit	*Credit*
Payroll Taxes Expense	_____	
FICA Tax Payable		_____
Medicare Tax Payable		_____
Unemployment Tax Payable – Federal		_____
Unemployment Tax Payable – State		_____

Date	Account Title and Explanation	Doc No.	Post. Ref.	General Debit		General Credit	
			JOURNAL				Page

NOTE: *This page may be removed from the LIFEPAC to make it easier to journalize and post these transactions.*

	JOURNAL						Page	
Date	Account Title and Explanation	Doc No.	Post. Ref.	General Debit		General Credit	

Account Title: Cash   Account No. 110

Date		Explanation	Post. Ref.	Debit		Credit		Balance Debit		Balance Credit	
Sept.	1		✔					41044	95		

Account Title: Employee Income Tax Payable   Account No. 210

Date		Explanation	Post. Ref.	Debit		Credit		Balance Debit		Balance Credit	
Sept.	1		✔							1959	00

Account Title: *FICA Tax Payable*   **Account No.** *220*

Date		Explanation	Post. Ref.	Debit		Credit		Balance			
								Debit		Credit	
Sept.	1		✔							1599	60

Account Title: *Medicare Tax Payable*   **Account No.** *230*

Date		Explanation	Post. Ref.	Debit		Credit		Balance			
								Debit		Credit	
Sept.	1		✔							347	55

Account Title: *Unempl. Tax Payable – Federal*   **Account No.** 240

Date 20—	Explanation	Post. Ref.	Debit	Credit	Balance Debit	Balance Credit
Sept. 1		✔				157 30

Account Title: *Unempl. Tax Payable – State*   **Account No.** 250

Date 20—	Explanation	Post. Ref.	Debit	Credit	Balance Debit	Balance Credit
Sept. 1		✔				996 60

Account Title: *U. S. Savings Bonds Payable*   **Account No.** 260

Date 20—	Explanation	Post. Ref.	Debit	Credit	Balance Debit	Balance Credit
Sept. 1		✔				350 00

Account Title: *United Way Payable*   **Account No.** *270*

Date 20—		Explanation	Post. Ref.	Debit		Credit		Balance			
								Debit		Credit	
Sept.	1		✔							114	00

Account Title: *Payroll Taxes Expense*   **Account No.** *550*

Date 20—		Explanation	Post. Ref.	Debit		Credit		Balance			
								Debit		Credit	

Account Title: *Salary Expense*   **Account No.** *570*

Date 20—		Explanation	Post. Ref.	Debit		Credit		Balance			
								Debit		Credit	